# *Laughing* CULT

# Laughing CULT

## KEVIN McCAFFREY

POEMS

─ FOUR WINDS PRESS ─

SAN FRANCISCO

Paperback ISBN: 978-1-940423-00-5
Ebook ISBN: 978-1-940423-01-2

Four Winds Press
San Francisco, CA
www.fourwindspress.com

Cover art: Matt Phillips, "Revolverlator (Ochre)," 2013, oil on canvas, 20" x 24". Photo by Adam Reich.
Cover design: Domini Dragoone
Interior design: Tabitha Lahr
Author photo: James Gehrt

*Do you want to change your results while leaving what you do more or less unchanged?*

For my mother, Phyllis McCaffrey

# Contents

Dinner with dad . . . . . . . . . . . . . . . . . . . . . . . . . . 1

Chute . . . . . . . . . . . . . . . . . . . . . . . . . . . . . . . . 3

I'll stay away from dallying . . . . . . . . . . . . . . . . . 5

Blame it on the lute . . . . . . . . . . . . . . . . . . . . . . 6

Doubting what I saw . . . . . . . . . . . . . . . . . . . . . 8

Attempting to know everything while
    hating McGee . . . . . . . . . . . . . . . . . . . . . . . . 10

Song . . . . . . . . . . . . . . . . . . . . . . . . . . . . . . . . 11

Speechifier . . . . . . . . . . . . . . . . . . . . . . . . . . . . 13

Fool's awakening . . . . . . . . . . . . . . . . . . . . . . . . 15

Lovett and his donkeys . . . . . . . . . . . . . . . . . . . . 16

Quasi-nonexistence through psychic fusion
    with an experience . . . . . . . . . . . . . . . . . . . . 18

Robot . . . . . . . . . . . . . . . . . . . . . . . . . . . . . . . 20

The sister I never had . . . . . . . . . . . . . . . . . . . . 21

When do we want it? . . . . . . . . . . . . . . . . . . . . 22

The priest melts down . . . . . . . . . . . . . . . . . . . . . . . 23

Laughing cult . . . . . . . . . . . . . . . . . . . . . . . . . . . . 25

My team . . . . . . . . . . . . . . . . . . . . . . . . . . . . . . . 27

Perfection . . . . . . . . . . . . . . . . . . . . . . . . . . . . . . 28

A rest stop for moles . . . . . . . . . . . . . . . . . . . . . . . 30

An astronaut resigns himself to love . . . . . . . . . . . . 32

A beast . . . . . . . . . . . . . . . . . . . . . . . . . . . . . . . . 33

Blind date with a king . . . . . . . . . . . . . . . . . . . . . . 34

How I lost faith in my inner voice . . . . . . . . . . . . . 35

Fawn . . . . . . . . . . . . . . . . . . . . . . . . . . . . . . . . . . 37

Anapestic approach in demand for
    this task . . . . . . . . . . . . . . . . . . . . . . . . . . . . . 38

Cliff leapers . . . . . . . . . . . . . . . . . . . . . . . . . . . . . 40

Ideas expressed in the school gym . . . . . . . . . . . . . 42

Staff art show . . . . . . . . . . . . . . . . . . . . . . . . . . . . 43

Is it me? . . . . . . . . . . . . . . . . . . . . . . . . . . . . . . . . 45

It's nothing . . . . . . . . . . . . . . . . . . . . . . . . . . . . . . 47

Mud season . . . . . . . . . . . . . . . . . . . . . . . . . . . . . 48

No problem . . . . . . . . . . . . . . . . . . . . . . . . . . . . . 51

Dobbs . . . . . . . . . . . . . . . . . . . . . . . . . . . . . . . . 52

Performance evaluation . . . . . . . . . . . . . . . . . . . . 53

Commissar unplugged . . . . . . . . . . . . . . . . . . . . . 54

Branch manager's admission . . . . . . . . . . . . . . . . 56

Mal's pal . . . . . . . . . . . . . . . . . . . . . . . . . . . . . . 57

Writing rondeaux . . . . . . . . . . . . . . . . . . . . . . . . 59

Philosophy du jour . . . . . . . . . . . . . . . . . . . . . . . 60

Ultimate repast . . . . . . . . . . . . . . . . . . . . . . . . . 63

Mechanical Nostradamus on
    New Year's Eve . . . . . . . . . . . . . . . . . . . . . . . . 65

At the very lengthy meeting . . . . . . . . . . . . . . . . . 67

Plea to the manager of a store that
    never opens . . . . . . . . . . . . . . . . . . . . . . . . . . 68

The easy way . . . . . . . . . . . . . . . . . . . . . . . . . . . 70

Be like the creek . . . . . . . . . . . . . . . . . . . . . . . . 72

Winter . . . . . . . . . . . . . . . . . . . . . . . . . . . . . . . 74


Notes . . . . . . . . . . . . . . . . . . . . . . . . . . . . . . . . 77

About the author . . . . . . . . . . . . . . . . . . . . . . . . 79

# Dinner with dad

*"What does the coyote want to do with his life?"*
    —Isabel Schimmers, *Conquering the Badlands with Magic*


It was the usual dinner with the usual questions
but when my daughter's new boyfriend told me
that, after college, he wanted to become a life
coach—a fucking consultant—to wild
animals, I had to restrain myself
from getting up wordlessly and walking
out. I could see my daughter's wariness,
watching me, watching him, for familiar signs
that something was going to go down like those unavoidable
days when the material and mystical worlds
rearrange themselves in their hallucinated games
of musical spheres. But I stayed on, molding
my face into a grimace-free visage,
bidding my passions to heel like dogs,
and asked this young Lothario how
he'd do what hadn't been done before,
at least so far as I remembered, excepting
for the sake of argument Orpheus and Francis
of Assisi as being the only two I knew
who'd done some similar shit with animals
and such. He countered with a life-strategy of
writing his own job description, following
his bliss, and maybe interning at a zoo or Sea-
World and then trekking into the wild like that dude

in the movie . . . "where his ass starved in the end?"
I butted in and he looked confused, then smiled, meek,
nodding yes, until my daughter, sleek,
moved in to rescue him like she'd rescued me
countless times before in the bad
old days, so I relented and the dinner
moved on and went just fine, I mean
as fine as these awkward dinners can go.

# Chute

My wife and son have left the house for a while,
how long they'll be gone I don't know—
the house is as still as my empty mind;
it takes on a shadowy glow.

Ticking clock and refrigerator hum—
these are the muted sounds I hear.
I have nothing to say to anyone.
Funny how that becomes more clear.

This basement is where I spend my time.
I like it because it is cool,
yet I use the hours when they are gone
to climb up through the laundry chute

to the lived-in rooms above my pit
where I can watch a little t.v.
and grab myself a beer, a snack, some chips—
feeling remnants of memories.

They flicker by, these memories—they glow
like particles of dust in light.
I can become transfixed by every mote,
dwell in diminishing delight

until my son and wife come bickering home,
then I descend, leaving scant trace
that I have pushed aside the spectral stone
once more to take my rightful place.

Sometimes they pause by the basement door
and gaze into the blackness here,
but both are reluctant to come below
to see who might have moved the chair

in the living room so slightly, or switched
the often broken toaster on.
Though there is no thief where there is no theft,
they are wary of my return.

# I'll stay away from dallying

It is like being halfway from the summer
house to the winter house and remembering
you've left the bongo drums behind
and, thinking yourself unwatched, throwing a
little fit, stomping and grouching and then
sensing the dispassionate observer in the corner of
the enclosure and feeling the embarrassment of being
seen, at least that is what some say
it's like, so I'll stay away from such activities
for now in the same way I avoid
other things, but when the all-clear
sounds, please stand aside, Plotinus,
I'll be on hand in an instant with all my capabilities,
fully slathered in unguents and perfumes—
I'll be a walking flower to be there
to savor such frolicsome dallying when I hear
that supergreen signal sound.

# Blame it on the lute

There's a salute to the Ute in Utah . . .
the kind of thing you can't avoid.
A salute to the Ute in Utah,
I've heard lutes are employed.

And when it's the gloaming in Wyoming,
there the lute figures heavily too;
what buffalo like when they're roaming
is the strum of the heavenly lute.

They're reading the *Dhammapada* in Nevada,
so their spirits are totally buoyed,
that and the lute's silky *cascada*—
all negative energy's destroyed.

The lute really kicks ass in Texas,
it was there when the Alamo fell;
eating marimbas and guitars for breakfast,
it blazed like the fires of Hell.

Oh, let's meet at the corner of Arizona
and three other southwestern states;
the lutists there are full grown—ah!—
that's why the Four Corners gyrate.

Did you hear tell of a tornado in Colorado,
how the lute was the cause of all that,
played by a musical desperado?
He played everything in B-flat.

They are staying flexible in New Mexico,
moved by the lute's ludic pulse,
dancing a gyrating do-si-do,
giving rein to every impulse.

Yes, the lute is the reason, through every season,
that certain western states give rein to every impulse.

# Doubting what I saw

The enemy of my enemy is
my friend, but what about his sister?
I'm not so sure of her. She passed by here
the other day, trailing vapors, mists, fizz . . .
she's ghostly . . . and I think she blew a kiss
to someone—not to a random mister
either; my memories are all astir,
but furtive kisses inform my thesis

as I recall her recent stroll to mind,
though recollections shift when scrutinized.
Sometimes they even die. They're euthanized
by stronger thoughts, and by the fact we're blind,
at least in part, to what we think. To find
out if this is true or not, utilize
your introspective powers, your mind's eyes,
to look inside your thoughts. They're ill-defined

at best, unruly shadows, faded, blurred,
and prone to hide or fabricate details.
Was the walking woman greeted or hailed
by someone hidden out of view, obscured,
who met her with a nod, a happy word,
an innocent hello? That is a tale
so much better than the doubt that assails
me now, that makes my thinking mind absurd.

For if she, sister to the enemy
of my most hated foe, has put aside
her love for me—and all her love implied—
and shifted it to him, given freely
what had infused my every fantasy
with pseudo-physicality, then chide
the fool who takes her for his ideal bride,
as if he knows his own reality.

# Attempting to know everything while hating McGee

If attempting to know everything (while hating McGee) is like
trying to know nothing, then put
me down for that approach and I'll clear my mind
like agriculturalists tidy a field, scything
and pulling until the ground is brown, see?
But if that doesn't work, why then
I'll drop napalm, God's finest
elixir, to burn my thoughts right down to gravy
nothings, my mellow harshed to the maximum—
gone, prettified, wan poser whose
game is wack like this incessant rain,
powerfully invisible from nothing clouds,
the drops checking every checkbox—
some answers must be right—
so you can't even see the mud or where it was.

Still, abruptly knowledge comes that
tasks have been left undone by the universe:
One thing is that it has not waterproofed all the shoes
it should have, so a lot of us, deluged,
will get seriously wet feet if we go out,
though only upstarts depart the ark.
So what else has Mr. Universe left undone?
He has left you alive, McGee. It's hard
for me to even think about knowing nothing
when I know that.

# Song

My fate and I walked side by side;
it was my shadow, though never spied.
Sometimes it followed, sometimes it led,
unseen companion from birth to death.

I did not know that it was there,
so quiet my fate was, transparent, clear,
yet it drove my existence from bad to worse;
I did not know my life was cursed.

The voice in my mind whispering advice
to do this or that when I faced a choice—
that was my fate, steering me wrong.
I could not resist it. How strong! How strong!

Who was it showed me I was in thrall
to a baleful deceiver, the tunes he called?
It was you, child, your second sight
showed me my fate, grim parasite.

You taught me to see it, this fevered ghost—
it was a fluke-worm and I the host.
You taught me to kill it, drive it away;
using your love, dear, I killed my fate.

Now I am boundless. Now I am free.
No furtive voices whisper to me.
What will my life hold, now that I am unchained?
Where will I go now that I'm unconstrained?

Untied, unfettered, I've made a new start.
I've slain the slick serpent that circled my heart.
False hates and fears I have escaped;
with your sweet love, girl, I killed my fate.

# Speechifier

Who is he? I mean the one who
influences us to do what
we do, who strums the collective lyre
our group-mind to incite, and who brews
the figurative concoction that
transmutes verbal into actual fires?

The answer is the speechifier.
Who knows how words can be like jewels
all strung together, pearls; or like a deck
of cards, turned as the game requires
to show patterns that boost or skew
our thrills; or like nicely drafted

images that, if drawn with craft,
compel aversion or desire
throughout the crowds that think they choose
all on their own to go to large museums? I speak, in fact,
of our national town crier,
noting his mean birth, humble youth,

his rise against odds, jumping through hoops,
his tumbling hard, his prospects wrecked,
his standing up, eyes aiming higher,
to give his first speech from his own stoop:
His words unfolded, rattled the air,
though none were there at that late hour

to see him gesture and perspire,
waving his arms as if the truth
were keen to do whatever he bid—
it has since done, or I'm a liar,
a hidden canyon packed with straw.
From stadium to polling booth,
from country farm to city flat

his is the voice, his the attack
that compels us, soothes, raises ire,
or whispers mild like pitching woo—
although his tone can hiss and rasp.
Where his words, his thoughts aspire,
that is where I'll go. And you?

The only truths are collective truths.
I feel we join in that instant—
shout with one mouth, sing as one choir—
when he speaks. All sprung from one root,
how smooth to pledge our joint consent
to do whatever his voice inspires.

# Fool's awakening

You'd spent the whole day trying
to write a really fine punk song
about whether flowers think or not,
but, hampered, you'd drunk a lot,
you met with periods of unclear
mentation, so you took some drugs in your fustian
frustration and lost yourself entirely in
the Arnold Arboretum, conking
out. Angelic hosts, you were en route
to see 'em, when you evacuated
all, using every fleshly avenue.
Let's give a shout-out to life-saving
puke, sweat, shit, snot, and drool. Piss too!
You awoke around dawn, befouled
and bedewed, yet, sagacious owl,
or maybe more wood-weasel's friend,
you perceived proximate a stagnant
pond and waded in to remove
what you could better do without.
So, peaceful feelings, serene warm dawn,
until a ranger's shouts chased you
back to your squalid punk rock prison,
ancient, dripping infant: botched baptism.

# Lovett and his donkeys

*"Although I looked down from high above, I saw clearly the round, earthbank-enclosed corral filled with many donkeys surrounding my friend Lovett who, wearing a cowboy hat, was pressed upon on all sides by the donkeys."*

—Isabel Schimmers, *Conquering the Badlands with Magic*

After I joined the charlatans' circle, I saw
exactly why the cake was half-baked
and why the fat lady would never
set foot on the stage of the situation
so that like, presumably, life itself,
it would unwind as a roll of sheet music—
given an effectively imagined mechanism—
for one of those endless, unlistenable operas
by one of those American maximalist composers
even though, speaking truth to power, I might expire
before any chance of hearing the grand finale
(just as audience members often outright
die enduring *Einstein on the Beach*), yet
the group told me there might be some solace
in exploring the shifting spaces between wakefulness
and sleep, so I gave it the old necromantic try
and I'll make some observations, the first of which is
watch out: when you point your broomstick
towards those wastes beyond the dunes, the sky, and the horizon
and fly for weeks in the frosty air

then almost any breeze or snatch of song
can carry you to wistful places,
haunted places, like that from which Lovett returned
oblivious, transformed, to promote a show
called *Donkeys Make the Man*
and had six episodes in the can and it was already
sold to a network after a bidding war—
and while this was admittedly a rare-cooked shank,
I was not in any way impressed by it.
I could see that he'd psychically left the circle
and I started to distance myself from him.

# Quasi-nonexistence through psychic fusion with an experience

I seek an experience so pure and powerful
that it will render me invisible
in that I will become that experience completely
(through psychic fusion or other mechanism
difficult to explain using our words)
and disappear with it into the shaded past
as it disappears—except perhaps from memory;
in that case, I will be remembered, though not for long.
Or in the case of fusion with an ongoing phenomenon—
one of expansive if not infinite duration,
then, though I will still exist, it will be
as though I've disappeared. I'll be subsumed
into something else. For the sake of argument,
I won't be here. I'll be French or something.

So today I plan to spend the hours
imagining the things with which I could
conjoin. Something fleeting as an April shower
or longer lasting: the hardness of a concrete tower;
a concept like hyperrealism or a belief,
theosophy, and I, though practically nothing,
could be both gone and present virtually
for quite some time, though really what
I'm thinking about can't be done
and while you won't hesitate to tell me

throughout the shoddy afternoon hours
that I'm still here, I won't be able to resist
reminding you that you don't exist either—
my imaginary critic, my posited Charles Simic—
since you chose to leave this ranch long ago
to go mining silver ore
in the drab hills of a fabricated Ecuador
where, according to some reports, you became
one with the silver sparkling under the earth.
Anyway, I never heard from you again.

# Robot

Sorry I have been quiet today, but you know
how I am. When I don't know what
to do I do nothing, just spending
time playing mind games
with you, friend, throughout the languid afternoon
until the long-awaited buzz of the
evening news and the two of us turn
to this something to do, to this not that much
but still something. The world is out there
just where it should be.

The mechanical wistfulness of your companionship tantalizes
me, yet I am not without self-doubt.
What is my life? Put on the music and
get the cards, Robot. Tonight
is the night we play for keeps.

## The sister I never had

She is the sister I never had, so
it may sound weird to say I married her . . .
incestuous almost . . . but it is not
like that, though actually if we had
been kin, foals of the same mare, to employ
your country terms, I would have married her
anyway, defying all convention,
ripping up the prohibition as Aldous
dismissed the covenant in the last act
of our national play, our epic, my
backwoods friends. So how would things be different
if we two were "whoopee twins" or "lustangs,"
to use again your rural phrases? I
wouldn't say she is the sister I never
had, for one thing. I'd be more circumspect.

# When do we want it?

*for Michelle Ducharme*

I've packed two pairs of shoes for the rally
and with what I've got on my feet, I've got six shoes.
It's a rally of ralliers, a ralliers' sally,
or attack, against that mother-loving empire of the blues
that keeps each of us from realizing what he needs as badly
as vaccine makers need the flu,
as carbonated drinks need spectral fizz.
In fact I can't wait to find out what it is

that I need really, though I think I need a sort of floppy dusk
that will permeate—no, wrong word—that will arrest
the flow of my life so that I'll always be on the cusp
of the passage between day and night, the crest
of a never-toppling wave. I'll discuss
this at the rally with the best
of the voices among the chanting crews:
Will there be someone there who wants to walk a mile in my shoes?

I bet there will be some fellow floppy duskers
to articulate our newly instantiated needs . . .
those who've envied how a butterfly hovers,
or how a moth, for that matter, under shadowy eaves
delays between one choice and another,
uncommitted as a judge facing equal pleas.
In twilight we'll march against tyrannical flux.
What do we want? Floppy dusk.

# The priest melts down

If believing there is no god
fulfilled like believing there is,
then my soul, if I had one,
would be calmer, more pacific.

To nothing I could pray and draw
solace from it; I'd be a pious
man, or a priest, in this new church,
telling my flock nothing forgives

your many sins, and no one cares
about your pains—and if people were
consoled by that, emboldened, braced,
then how much would it matter whether

there is a god or not? Not that
it seems to matter anyway.
Even if you think there is nothing
out there, no cosmic force, no ray

of light that launched all this for love,
is it good to pray, to pretend
that things are different? I've tried it.
For a moment I may feel intense

sensations—see, grasp, and hear things
enriching, sweet, surpassing fair,
but giving prayer a chance does
not mean there is much chance for prayer.

That's what I've found, after preaching
for a lifetime from this pulpit.
I've come to know mine is a creed
that has nothing going for it.

What urges me to share these thoughts—
courage or something worse? We'll see.
If unbelief can sustain faith,
my sheep, you will still follow me.

A universe without meaning
holds one sure thing, one certainty:
though mistrust me for the liar
I am, this truth won't set you free.

# Laughing cult

*"I write to let you know why I was yelling outside your apartment today . . . "*

—Personal notes and letters of Isabel Schimmers

A laughing cult moved in next door
exactly thirteen months ago.
They laugh throughout the circling hours—
"hee-hee" all day, all night "ho-ho."

What instigates such silly spirit
perplexes me. It perturbates
my soul. If you want to hear it,
come round my rooms when it grows late,

for that is when the general
carnival of unbridled glee
works itself to a bacchanal
of limitless hilarity.
You can't help but hear it through the walls.

And then we two can speculate
why these damn fools are laughing so—
they just can't wait to ululate—
but what the joke is I don't know.

I stopped a laugher on the street
and asked him what they're laughing at.
The interchange was incomplete—
mute silence was what I got back.

How about if I joined, I bluffed,
became a novice in the sect;
but my entreaty was rebuffed,
my crafty, furtive gambit checked

by a blank look. I don't wonder
for whom the bell tolls—that is known—
or why lightning comes with thunder.
The question that weighs like a stone

that's tied to a water-logged corpse
is what is the unending joke
that makes them laugh until they're hoarse?
What funny gods have been invoked
to hold this laughing cult in thrall?

# My team

My team plays in silence, the players holding
their tongues throughout the contest; never do
they shout, or taunt, or grunt, or moan. They speak
through action, symbolically. Tackles made
in the open field, interceptions, sweeps, trap-blocks,
and all the other facets of the sport, precise
in execution: this is how my team
communicates; and always violence
informs their silent diction, punctuated
by hitting. When with full force the body
of a running back is drummed to the ground,
or a wide receiver grasped in midair
and thrown with such might the ball pops from his hands
and he cries out, the wind knocked out of him—
these suffice, these are sounds enough for
my silent team, my mute professionals
for whom the wailing crowd is an intrusion
into the brutal reticence of soil, grass,
leather, wind, snow—they only hear the silence
that quarterbacks each violent play.

# Perfection

You are a restaurant reviewer for
the local weekly and a friend asks you
to review his restaurant and you agree
reluctantly. When you are there you see
the cook inadvertently spits in the food.
What do you do? If I told you there's
a pill you can take, made from rarest herbs,
that will ensure that whatever you do will
turn out perfectly—but only if you take
it in the right setting and in the right way—
would you be interested? Naturally
you would. A second case to further make
the point: who would not rather be the awkward
admirer of the icy beauty queen
whose stuttering approach results—against
all odds—in consummation? How? She's tired
of all the guys who couldn't care less about her mind;
somehow she reads your bumbling as true love.
And why is that? No need for speculation!
The peerless pill is doing what it does—
based, as it is, on ancient Taoist lore
juiced with biochemical enhancements
and certain Soviet mind-control advances—
and so the question: Do you want to change
your results while leaving what you do more
or less unchanged? There is no need to worry

further about your lack of talent or skill.
The answer's in my hand. The perfect pill.
Take it with me now and things will go right
for us.

# A rest stop for moles

Muse, please stop harrying me—
I am pretending as best I can that the place
where I work is not some tepidly surreal Hades,

but still you buffet me with idiocies . . .
it's becoming harder to nod and smile
as if I work in a crucial vending machine

doing important things—which I don't,
which you know, exacting Muse. I play
a role in dispensing candy to the moles

who happen to be tunneling nearby and take
a break for something sweet. It's not even
good candy. Today you used

your awesome power to make me chair
of a committee to study planting our machine
six-feet deep. Would it increase

business? The relocation committee will study this and
if you thought about it, Muse, you'd know our motto
is "excavation, excavation, excavation." I almost died

when I suggested that, even though all
the committee members laughed. And I know
that you're trying to make me quit my job

so I can write better poems for you,
but, Muse, that I can't do unless
you absolutely break my life in two.

Give it more effort, hallucinogenic Goddess,
or leave me alone. Why can't you just
accept my mediocre output? I do.

I'm just a tiny fellow in a vending machine.

# An astronaut resigns himself to love

We could have done this thing my way and ripped
her from the portal where she'd limped, then doused
her mercilessly, drenching her with washes
of liquidated time to show our friend
the mystery of her sense of self and what
that indicated—and naturally to add
a touch of goblin music to the mix
would have ensured results as is well known
to everyone but you apparently;
instead you chose untried approaches that,
if we inhabited a moonscape of dreams,
would work just fine, but here where mud, when wet,
still sticks if thrown, I mean thrown hard, against
a wall or better yet a statue named
"New Ways of Doing Things," the way you tried
to make things clear, so clear a child could see,
has scripted patterns to her sense by which
she will elude all clarity and stay.
She, who if left alone would have attained
her own sure knowledge that she had to go,
will never leave the station now, but binds
our two unwilling bodies with her gravity.
The manual warns us astronauts of
the hazards born of giving space to love—
she joins us in our orbits of ourselves:
weightless as we are, there is no counterforce.

# A beast

A beast wanted to be a beast no more
and sought out hunters who'd capture him
and bring him back to this small city's zoo.
We went and saw the creature, of course not
knowing each other then, and met outside
the cage where a sign announced: "This beast
wants to be in this zoo. So there!" He met
our gazes with slow-moving eyes and roared
with pleasure, I thought. You said he looked bored.

You and I were the only people who
went to see the beast that afternoon, though
the new attraction was hyped by the zoo
in every way, but our prime fascination
was with each other, and leaving the zoo
we've remained together for years and years.
So, I was the beast who came willingly
to your zoo and you were the beast who came
willingly to mine and if this is not
the most remarkable tale in the world,
let it go back to the jungle of all
the things you've never heard. It does not need
to come in from the wild.

# Blind date with a king

Your tongue is better than plain and your nose
is a powderpuff on an inviting
field. Your ears, cheeks, hair, neck, arms, torso
are all quite nice. The softness of your skin
is more than is expected or even
hoped for. You, girlfriend-of-our-future, boast
other features too, fitting in a queen.
In thought, demeanor, mood, you're the most, but
your eyes, your crazily wandering eyes,
look at us the wrong way, near perfect thing,
and the chill we feel is as nonbinding
as exposure to plain cuisine in any

arctic clime, so that your eyes, we beg you,
you must shut behind dark lenses and, dousing
those hideous suns, struggle if need be—
even sightless—though oh-so-strong of mind.
When your eyes have become vassals to our care,
then we may move on. We will take you where
you want to go, even if you must go blind.

# How I lost faith in my inner voice

I'll stop listening to the voice in
my head if you stop listening to yours
and I'll stop writing down what it says, too, Philip,
as if it has some sort of deep significance.
There, in the ponderous whisperings between
my ears, I always thought insights were to be heard,
but maybe I was wrong about this, wrong
as is almost my hobby, wrong in everything,
unlike you, I know, who're always so right—
right in the morning right in the evening
and so on and so on until the day you're wrong
and take a page out of my book and wear
my moccasins—but back to what's at hand:
through focusing attention and deeming
my inner voice oracular, enraptured, I
recorded its every word and marveled how
its bland, convincing tone reminded me
somehow of Andy Warhol—listless, fey,
a puerile Sybil fully gassed, entranced,
delivering profundities that were,
it finally hit me, not that deep. I thought
this voice to be my true voice, that which speaks
at the very core of my so-called self:
my all-American, red-white-and-blue
voice . . . well, if not quite that—it *was* Warholian,
and who thinks of him as wrapped in the flag? . . .

at any rate it spoke to me, this voice—
alluring, charming, soft—effusing thoughts
like: "I want to learn the ways of smoke
and follow smoke into the hills," or this:
"What kinds of sounds do your animal selves
unleash when they are freed?" These utterances
enthralled me for years until something
about this inner voice, its snaky sibilance
I guess, began to make me think these were
mere fabrications, forms without substance,
fantastic words that, simulating truths,
were high in fat and low in actual meat;
strangely, the dictum that sealed the deal
began: "I'll stop listening to the voice in
my head if you stop listening to yours."
It was the kind of thing I'd heard before
and so have you if you've listened to me—
it just becomes less convincing over time.

# Fawn

Fawn, I am stupid in your presence and
in the moving forest passengered with animals.
What? What is nature between us?
Is it dowdy? Fawn, is it? There is
a certain way the brook moves—it chides
tectonic platitudes, sliding, wanton,
wandering. Lassitude in other words,
friendly fawn, a way we could share,
though we two are nervous in the service
of this gloomy counterintuitive wood.
Why did the maker make me me
and you you? With this question am I chilled
in the gnostic cooler of the expandable.
If I run after you, we both know what you'll do,
but will you do it like you mean it?
I do not think I could chase you in an authentic way.

# Anapestic approach in demand for this task

The unending unfoldings of dastardly plots,
intermixed with ineptitude, malice, and lust—
all the worst of the qualities making the men
of this region incredibly loathsome—result,
at the end of the story, in nothing. A book
on this place, not yet written, but covering all
that's transpired would require an infinity (more,
while it's hard to imagine) of words; and the need
for repeat situations, recurring unchecked
(all involving unsavory characters—men
in whom duty, endurance, civility, strength
of conviction, and other respectable traits
don't exist), for recyclings of similar themes
(as a clock through all time will revisit its hours),
and for patterns whose skew is more vapid than bad
would necessitate prose so devoid of élan
that a mild and undisciplined chronicler'd die
in attempting the narrative. Listlessness rules.

And while Fate has decreed that this land has had zilch
to impart in the general scheme of such things,
somehow I, having tenuous ties to this place
through my ancestors, real or surmised, am to find
the authorial voice who, undaunted by deep
exploration of wearisome evil, is set
to unveil this mundane, unforgivable land

to the world. As to how this dispatches me here
to your door, that's the question. Your faculty, ma'am,
for endurance is clear in considering what
you've produced. You alone can present the account
through circuitous weavings of falsehood and fact.
Compensation'll be bountiful though you must use
the contorted approach we employ in our speech:
anapestic throughout. In this way we'll produce
understanding, though subtle, of why we exist.
We're a people both dull and malignantly glib.

# Cliff leapers

A smattering of logs obscures the path
but my friend Walt Whitman is undaunted;
he leaps them—gone woodsman!—while I walk 'round.
The cliff's ahead where the prospect kicks ass,
Walt says, but my pet lemming's looking haunted.
He sees my saxophone—he hates the sound—

and the tape recorder hanging from my
shoulder and he knows that an art project
"à la the '70s" is in the works.
Well, the leashed lemming'll only get older
if we don't act is how I suggested
it to Walt this morning. We laughed like jerks

then but we both know the lemming won't jump
alone; Walt will jump with him, be unhurt,
then ascend again, cradling the lemming—
he's made of rubber maybe or the soul stuff
he speaks of so often in the verses
he intones nonstop whether I'm taping

or not. Anyway, as with certain folk,
his voice is pleasant even if you can't
figure what in heck he's really saying
more than half the time, though, this is no joke,
when we get to the clifftop—with cows like ants
below—the lemming looks like he is praying,

he's quiet and his eyes are closed, while Walt
grows ponderous, his beard flapped by the breeze,
and he allows as to how I should leap
too, taping and tooting as I vault
with them into the abyss; he calls me
"mate" and "o captain, my captain" and weeps

and hugs me close until, to be honest,
I'd rather jump than be squeezed, so I do.
As we fall together—saxophonist,
lemming, peerless bard—I just wish I knew:
if, when you die in a dream, you're gone,
what happens when you die in a poem?

# Ideas expressed in the school gym

I saw Joe the other day at the gym.
He's a sculptor, a professor of art,
and the idea I gave him was this:
I'd like to see a brain in a vat,
floating in some clear but oily liquid
and to the brain a wire would be attached
leading to a speaker, though Joe thought it'd
be better to have a telephone, black,
which, when viewers picked it up, would emit
the sound I'd been thinking of—a soft "ahh"
moaned endlessly from this organ in bliss.

Then Joe reminded me of another
idea I'd suggested in years gone by:
we should build an exit ramp to nowhere
veering off from Lower Lake Road to rise
and terminate abruptly in midair
over the shallow pond there; large green signs'd
be necessary—"Bear Right to Go Where
No One Goes"—to keep cars from taking dives.
To see a scale model of this concept
would be in and of itself a delight,
I told Joe, noting that, as a member
of the campus landscape committee,
moving this forward was in his purview
and that he had the clout to make it fly.

# Staff art show

The only thing better than not doing
something well is not doing it at all
and the next best thing to that is screwing

it up completely so that it does not
come off as even a half-assed attempt
put forward by a half-wit or wing-nut,

like when someone who, for instance, can't paint
sets out with best intent to sketch a scene
in oils but since Grandma Moses he ain't—

to employ slang—my pet orangutan
could do better; you get the picture, I
hope: it's embarrassing, though not the same

as what results from efforts of dabblers,
hobbyists, and amateurs who never
fail to miss the mark. These vain mishandlers

get it just a little bit wrong. So who
will tell them that a failure's a greater
failure to the extent it comes close

in the same way nearly great orators
are worse than verbose? Where's the pompous,
self-loathing, hectoring poetaster

who'll play the role of the disparager?
Not me. I am a participant
and expect to be the second place winner,
at least.

# Is it me?

I have brilliant ideas and sometimes
I forget them only to find myself
thinking them again. Here's an example:
about a year ago it came to mind
that having my portrait done—if wealth
wasn't an object (my ego is ample

enough!)—would be a kick and a half, but
only if I were painted as a corpse
laid in an open coffin to be viewed
before burial, my body trashed, shut
down completely. Perhaps I'd look older,
shriveled with age, or sick and greenish hued,

my flowing curls ghost white, my lips set firm
into a sort of Mona Lisa smile.
I told this idea to Bonnie, who paints
and also works at my office. She spurned
the thought, didn't think patrons would queue for miles
to pose and pay for their hip death portraits.

So the idea itself died: first obscure,
as soon forgot; no mental funeral
marked its annihilation from my thoughts,
until cerebral resurrection stirred
and, like Duchamp finding the urinal—
actually, not like that at all—hot,

driving to Lee the day before the Fourth,
the windows down in the Civic, I told
my girlfriend Lesleigh how neat it could be
to make photos of models feigning death,
but this didn't come out of nowhere: it flowed
from a chat about graveyards and rubbing

old gravestones we'd been having. She'd Googled
the process, prompted by an excursion
we'd made the day before to cemeteries
in Pelham and New Salem—quaint, frugal
expanses. Anyway, her aversion
to the shoot-them-as-if-they're-dead series

was clear. "I think it's morbid and perverse,"
she said, adding nothing more. I didn't speak
either, somewhat floored, even almost gored
by her words—her a bullock with a purse
and me a matador for whom critique
is piercing—and then feigning being bored,

I said, "But I'm morbid and perverse. Is
that, uh, something you don't like about me?"
"I'm not sure," she replied, not at all flip
but matter of fact, though what was cursed was
the hush that stretched on and on as no wry
retort or quip came to my deadened lips.

# It's nothing

From nowhere came this special type of nothing
to hang unsensed above the signal sectors
of our life and then to twine invisibly,
reaching through every room in this our spacious
suburban home, making of each a chamber
less superb somehow than in earlier days
when light and shadow rallied here. But let's
be honest: nothing noticeably changed
that much except the time the legs were pulled
out from under the velvet easy chair
and it collapsed—unnerving incident
that fairly gasped, now in retrospect,
how things were going flat and there was nothing
we could do even if we tried. I guess
the moral of the story is when someone
you love sighs "oh, it's nothing," then beware—
it just might come to nothing after all.

# Mud season

"Besides rocketing off the planet, you
can do almost anything to get high,"
Owen said. "My brother, when he is blue,
does algebra until his mind is fried."
"Dude!" I said. Then I said it again: "Dude!"
as we left Brewster where Owen let fly
the pass of his career . . . until gusts blew
it from Winslow's hands—a noble try
for he was no quarterback type. Aloof,
we three would've let the ball he'd launched just lie
where it'd plopped on snowy grass, but whoosh:
wind blew, ball rolled downhill to Swamp, and eyes
had it no more, so that was all we knew

of Weatherbie's kid's football's fate and why,
when the forgotten ball turned up anew
as we three stoned rubber-booted fools vied
to cross the Swamp next mud season, Winslow
hooted with hilarity. His surprise
was mystically unsettling; he threw
back his head and "An elf did this," he cried,
cackling so loud that heads across campus turned,
brows furrowed, ears cocked, and eyes opened wide—
and even if this is not strictly true,
I recall it as I recall his tries
to pry the ball from mud that held like glue
until a liquid sucking sound, a sigh

in reverse, signaled the pulling was through.
And Winslow admired the ball, his trophy,
though besmirched with grime and deflated too
(much like a muscle which had atrophied,
losing size); he raised it high and, imbued
with mischief akin to an elf or sprite's,
intoned these lines: "My dearest friends, it should
be clear that, just as in *Lord of the Flies*,
we pampered boys have left our pampered world
to come to this world of mud." In this wise
he droned on unmesmerizingly, but
what made us look at him was how he wiped
mud from the ball as he spoke and rubbed
on his tennis sweater a rough brown stripe
and daubed his cheeks and dabbed his nose with mud
as he stepped on a stump, where from on high
he said, "Hail, God of Mud, we bow to you,"
then tossed Owen the quasi-orb, muddy
still—an ill-fated lateral which due
to Owen's aversion—he stepped aside—
splashed and bobbed in the stream, that silty stew,
before the current took it in its stride
and rushed with it. So, how could we not muse
at the ball's improbable history
and likely fate: the Pond and then who knew—
first the Merrimack, then the sea's storied
expanses? But we didn't. We didn't value
knowing where the ball went, so we didn't spy
Weatherbie's kid dashing down to the brook

nor him using a stick to catch and guide
his lost ball to the bank. "Dudes," I said, "look!"
when I saw—for something had drawn my eyes—
the boy's run, complete with feints and jukes,
the ball in the crook of his arm, knees high;
a dance piece of celebratory moves
marked his triumph when he crossed his goal line
at Brewster. Owen yawned; Winslow approved,
cried out, "The God of Mud has set things right."
"Dude!" I nodded. Then I exulted: "Dude!"

# No problem

The problem is there is no problem and
the problem solvers have nothing to do
so they start creating problems out
of thin air, out of nothing. Then the problem
is not to see that there are big problems
everywhere and it is woe unto
him or her who cannot see or who will
not acknowledge the problems—they become
part of the problem, a big part of it,
their apathy or obstinacy holding
progress back until they are educated
to the fact that, one, there are big problems,
and, two, if you are not part of solving
them then you represent the problem
the problem solvers have been talking about
all along. So you see now how it is:
there is no problem worse than no problem.

# Dobbs

"Report," I'd said to Captain Dobbs, "report!"
and his report was good—I mean to say
it was a full report about a sticky
situation—plainly reasoned, graphed . . .
not that we were in any mood for laughs
since things up there were melting down and soon
the same was headed here. So what, I probed,
was his advice to us in these last hours
before oblivion: to seek refuge—
there was nowhere to go—or kneel and plead
as if some loving god might intervene,
or acquiesce, accepting fate, or run
amok like oils now free of past constraints,
brushes gone wild? In sum, what were his views?

"Sir, that exceeds the scope of my report,"
said Captain Dobbs and fixed me with a look
I couldn't read—and still can't—but I thought,
if any of us might, Dobbs would pull through.
I was wrong. Only I got out alive,
though Dobbs held on as long as anyone
and would have made the launch, the blurred escape,
if he had not slipped on a tube of paint.

# Performance evaluation

Maybe the kinds of things I am trying
to do are not the kinds of things I want
to do and that is why my performance,
while generally fine, is lacking in
enthusiasm. Some call me even-keeled;
my bearing's understated, muted, bland,
and in my inner mental life—my mind
in other words—it's much the same: the flame
is turned to low so that "the pumpkin's cooked
inexpertly," to quote the chef from near the patch
in Fairy Glen whose pies were deemed expressive
of all that comes from vegetables grown
in the cool soil of lengthy nights. Just say
the dial is set to low in the oven
of my mind, which, to start another thread
(while putting one bad metaphor to bed),
is filled with half a dozen feelings and
maybe a hundred thoughts which recur
in finite patterns like an irksome fugue,
so that the thinker—me—is bored. Thus, it's
not the job alone, Mr. Newlin, sir,
it's how the job and I combine that is
a matter for our mutual concern.

# Commissar unplugged

You wonder what had happened to the message
in its encoded transit from transmitted
to received, its code intact, the system clean?
What happened was an alteration in
the meaning to something absurd, so "we
attacked and lost entire battalions of
choirboys and Chihuahuas; the valiant hymns,
the fervid barkings made a difference not
at all. The singing ended with a boom,
while tiny dogs embraced their dooms"—
some one had blunder'd, or that's what we thought
at first. We even shot a man before
we reappraised—now he's a hero of
the Ceaseless Revolution—but as to
the more important point, our analysts
finally found no human fingerprint,
no interaction whatsoever in
the incident. The words transformed themselves.

Once would have been enough—but when is it
in these times when the falcon cannot hear
the falconer and not because he's deaf,
to make a joke from out of our bourgeois past?
The Leader called on us to do what we do:
my team devised a theory that appears
to stand up well. To oversimplify,

our thinking holds that long exposure to
technology results in unexplained
twistings in meanings over time, or "words
plus digitization plus transmission all
add up to we are screwed," according to
the formula our crack decoder screamed
before we had to take him out and shoot
him too, for therapeutic reasons, one
can be assured, my Comrades. It is all
elaborated fully, set before
you on your desks in my account. Please note
that since it's copied out by hand it stands
more chance of being true. I sing the word
unelectrified, if you'll indulge me one
last time before you pull my plug. In short,
my Leader, we have failed to find out how
to force our words back to what once they were:
usually static if untouched by guile,
tending to constancy despite our wiles.

# Branch manager's admission

"There may be some delay between the time
a deposit is made and when it is
posted to your account," she screamed, then fell,
to writhe, contorted, moaning, totally freaked—
a teller whose work will need to be addressed
by someone. But not me. Though I manage
the bank I rarely take what might be deemed
decisive action. "Blessed are the meek"
is my motto and it has served me well
in my slow rise from trainee to manager
here at the Bartleby Bank and Trust,
where I am paid to hide my feelings and
the more I hide them, the more I'm paid.

# Mal's pal

Hoboes with oboes can
play some swinging low notes, Flann;
but if you think that you'd bestow
lower blows than this hobo,

get your instrument unhooked,
trot out to the hobo's wood—
scattered tones will guide your trip,
made by those hep to what's unslipped.

Mountainmen have flipped their crowns
beyond those badlands outside town—
sounds unfurl there, windy banners,
where he eviscerates the standards.

Useless are descriptive phrases . . .
just dig how he queers the changes.
Systematic, slyly free—
atavist, he riffs on "Cherokee."

When he plays the highest notes,
makes the yardbirds jump the moat,
asks who's first—chicken, egg?—
he's the one who pulls your leg.

Take it on to Middle Earth . . .
calculate this wizard's worth,
this Frodo's gone—in the flow—
hobo hobbiting his oboe.

Or like Charlie Chaplin armed,
ax in hand and doing harm,
so this hobo's bag is rarefied,
transcendent, Flann, knocked aside

like you took what Moderns dug,
turned it sideways with a shrug—
hobo, oboe's hegemon,
boplicitous, the real broke gong.

# Writing rondeaux

Writing rondeaux and rolling blunts,
spitting, stuttering, pulling stunts,
prescient like Nostradamus—
posers pleading "please don't harm us."
I'm spraying syllables, six-gun

shooting epithets when I hunt
second-class rhymesters, hip-hop runts—
the fact is it's time to practice
writing rondeaux.

Fence swinger, I'm hitting home runs,
bench sitter, you're laying down bunts;
you're baffled—what separates us?
My speed. I'm a rabbit like Bugs
Bunny, Elmer, leaving you stunned,
writing rondeaux.

# Philosophy du jour

Ever since I've become a Buddhist, I've started
to be a little easier on myself and build my
life more by taking things away than adding
them on. And so the emotional baggage
I've carted with me for these thirty-six years

is still here, piled high, but rolling more
smoothly, in case you wanted to know . . . which
hopefully you don't. Here is just another dilemma
for a guy like me who wants to bore deep
into his life without giving too much away,

without confessing, because confession
is difficult first but then becomes, like
therapy, too easy. Sure, when I
think about my life, it's a succession
of failures baffled sometimes by a marvelous

change. And, unlike you, my shame
has colored who I am, made my soul a
sort of green clay so that there is always
sadness in me, always a heavy expectancy
beneath the topsoil and vivid flowers, but

to dig it up to write it down seems weak.
Is that too harsh? It's just that in these
times everyone has suffered something so
unspeakable that all they do is speak
about what went wrong to shape them wrong—

about how strength starts with finding and securing
their fragility. I begin with myself too
and often what I write is based in the facts
of my life but changed and obscured
with lies. So, is this a way to make

something whole from my incompleteness
or simply to hide who I am from you? Or
is it that, mysteriously, the written word
has independent truth? Now that's
an assertion that's marked by overreach.

I will, in my newfound philosophy, which
sets right speaking within a noble truth, try
through meditation to dig to my root and then,
easy in my dishonesty, despising sympathy,
write something that is not me for you.

When I meditate, I sit in front of a wall.
My shadow's there. And in my slowing mind
sometimes thoughts wriggle and unwind
like roots and a stem from a flower's bulb,
shaping strange mental images undefined

by hard reason—funny thoughts such as
of a man whose nose is attached to a cloud or,
surreal and sad, of pregnancy's tremors
as I give birth to my own heart, freeing
what is best in me from the failure, at least

thus far, of my life, and impassively, with
closed eyes, see my heart as a child newborn
and hear its beat as cries of neither scorn
nor resignation, but of a simple need to live.
It does live and I live, less far gone

than in many years. Why? All credit to the
Buddha . . . or you if you'll take it, aware
that my praise is heavier than blame. If I am
prone to move from failure to failure, there's
merit in slowness I'll say, if I have to explain.

# Ultimate repast

*An advertising jingle for two voices*

If you dine at our restaurant—
*lucky man—*
savor every forkful of the meal
and report to our waitstaff—
*if you can—*
exactly what it makes you feel.

If you sup at our establishment—
*much ballyhooed—*
delight in every drop you quaff;
recount to me, your gracious host—
*don't be rude—*
precisely why it makes you laugh.

And if you sense that you can't speak—
*honored guest—*
muted by a thickening tongue;
your experience is not unique—
*I confess—*
our meals can strike a diner dumb

and make your hair throw off its snood—
*hurrah! hurrah!—*
and keep you rooted to your chair;
like a ship in the Horse Latitudes—
*blah blah blah—*
you'll stay put for lack of air.

Our restaurant is hard to find—
*well-born son—*
though seekers locate it at the end,
the final rest stop of the mind—
*walk, don't run—*
situated where all roads wend.

And if your senses start to flit—
*Heaven knows!—*
sights and sounds diminishing,
just order seconds of dessert—
*the meal's close—*
the time has come for finishing.

If you dine at our restaurant—
*dear Madam—*
savor every morsel of the meal
and depend on me, your maître d'—
*what a plan!—*
to make your experience ideal.

To serve the ultimate repast—
*not a boast—*
flesh, fish, and fowl cooked with perfect skill,
eternal moments meant to last—
*hungry ghost—*
so eat as if it is your final meal.

# Mechanical Nostradamus on New Year's Eve

In humor a new era starts,
a cosmic joke, the kind of laugh
the devil has, a sacrifice,
a curse, as when your robot slave

brought you a cup of tap, not bottled,
water and you required he drink
it down to punish his dysfunction.
Since *his* maker gave him no mouth,

he could but pour the water on
himself, honoring your injunction.
But that was just another glitch
for us, and so we'll leave it behind,

preprocessing what looms ahead,
a final chapter to this Age
of Iron. We will make a joke—
a robot-monkey fusion wearing

bell-bottomed jeans—of this new year.
In the year 2013
our metal selves will hum—coal-stoked!
Our algorithms will be pristine.

With humor this new era starts,
rebooting with a robot's laugh.
Though we'll have no use for human sense
in the soft logic of our mirth,

so little use for human sense,
as we ungag a laughing earth.
Let our metallic flagons clink—
imagined drinks! We'll learn to laugh.

# At the very lengthy meeting

At the very lengthy meeting
I actually felt my soul leave my body
and rush toward the ceiling—
and fly around the walls and flare
toward daylight, toward the windows—
to throw silently its impetuous emptiness
against the glass in vain.
It could not go anywhere, the clear moth.

Then it lay on the rug, not exhausted
but bored and so inert that it almost—
though nothing—
took on a hue, stained with all the breaths
and words and thoughts that filled the room:
the yellow-green color of old teeth.

# Plea to the manager of a store that never opens

*"Les non-dupes errent."*
　　—Jacques Lacan


You manage a store that never opens.
The wares displayed on darkened shelves include
masks, bracelets, drums, statuettes, and blowguns—
a head-hunting celebration only viewed
through a window that, in sum, betokens
the business model at your store is skewed
against commerce, against letting today's man
formulate and then execute a plan

to start hunting heads in this college town
for example, which, at any rate, would
be impractical and extreme, though sounds
of drumming can occasionally be heard
when drum circlers hold their weekly hoedowns
on the town common—rare, unhunted birds—
they're friends, neighbors, these pampered atavists
who are working out issues and seeking bliss.

It's obvious whatever bliss they find
won't come from shrinking someone's severed head.
That's why I want to get inside the minds
of those outmoded warriors whose dread,

whose joy—whose worldview—however unrefined,
is something we—unnerved through time—have shed
in becoming emasculated, bored,
modern men. Manager, open your store.

# The easy way

Your fantasies will not only come to nothing but will play
a part in drawing you from what was to be
the far easier fate that would have lain
in wait for you, a fate that was machine-milled and—
while not glimmering, for the finish was muted intentionally—
inspected by elves who shook, prodded,
bent, and probed it according to procedures
set out in the Trilogy itself and so I take it
very seriously that you, flushed with one victory,
rush to replace what was to be with what
won't work out so well.

Was it an unconscious impulse driving
your Volvo towards the house where your ex still lives?
Or was it hubris? You imagined yourself a modern Mars?
Or better yet, the influence of dour Lautréamont
(who'll take a cub and rearrange its spots)
drew you to automatize your actions as if you had no will,
which you did, prompting feelings, recriminations, screams,
and tears. Your fantasies are not your friends.

Whether in death or life, at toil or play,
whether here in Houston or in the hills, brown now,
whether chased or giving chase, let it be easy.
And the easiest way is when you identify your fate
and follow it like a shadow, a shadow which never has had

or will have a bad day, for who's heard
of an unwilling or unhappy shadow?
Whether hard or soft, remunerated or impecunious,
whether electrified or powerless—the system's down now—
whether chirpy, voiceless, informed, choiceless,
whether simple like Sunday morning, early,
or as convoluted as any drudging day at work
in an office of trolls, why not let it be easy?

# Be like the creek

Why do I make the promises I make,
speaking sleek words and lovely, sugared vows?
I am adept at making useless phrases
up on the spot to get me through the "now"—
as for follow through . . . that's a risk I'll take,
inventing as I go, letting things flow
naturally, or not, to their conclusion,
trusting organizational confusion

to keep me riding high. In general,
I tell you what you want to hear and then
do nothing, trusting in the ephemeral
nature of management's requests, and when
specific goals resurface—cast a pall
at sessions where a manager upends
the normal scheme and asks if something's done—
it's then, pacific, I unleash my tongue . . .

What will it say? It's odd: I rarely plan
or try to mold or shape the words I speak . . .
they bustle forth like bloodhounds from their van,
brought to a crime scene by hurried police
to sniff the trail, still fresh, of a wanted man
who has escaped the forest in a jeep.
Though focused as these eager dogs may be,
they scramble in this instance aimlessly.

Of their dogged persistence now I sing,
of how these purposeful, luckless searchers
could illustrate themes from the *Tao Te Ching,*
a tome that's hard to understand, for sure.
To boil down, crassly, its subtle teaching:
If doing nothing is what you treasure,
run barking through the office if you must—
say anything to keep your master's trust.

But you're not a dog, you say . . . you're human
and, like New Hampshire, either dead or free.
You won't put on airs, you're unassuming,
in no way practiced in hypocrisy.
There is so much that you could be proving
to those above you in the hierarchy.
That's great! You'll see, as your career unfolds,
the wages paid to the direct, the bold.

Those atavistic sages saw that soft
as water is, it gnawed through rock, reduced
all things to mud or sand, so let's not scoff
at how a babbling tongue, much like a brook,
can cut through—or around—whatever's tossed
in its path. It has no mandate to produce
value. It runs, not knowing what it seeks,
not knowing what it says. Be like the creek.

# Winter

Winter arrives with gifts of art, says
little sounds like paper being torn.
My lungs, my heart are lonely in my chest,
triplets waiting to be born

to life, death . . . the future is obscure—
an unrealized present shrink-wrapped in snow as
my insides are wrapped by flesh and bone.

Now the light of winter frolics
blue and handsome in instant cubes and
the air is purer, the sky's
lack of lacking and its birds suggest,

"hey, seek purity in the drifts."
What are these figures anyway? Snow-
covered bushes, children, squatting men . . .
Spring will flush, flesh them out
with heat and rain.

# Notes

A number of these poems have appeared on the *Exquisite Corpse* website. I first read of the wood-weasel—mentioned in "Fool's awakening"—in a poem of that name by Marianne Moore with the notable ending: "Only wood-weasels shall associate with me." The term "supergreen" used in "I'll stay away from dallying" comes from the movie *The Fifth Element*. Technically, I don't think "Mal's pal" played the oboe professionally. Thanks to Lesleigh Brisson and to my many friends who have been kind enough to read and offer thoughts on these poems.

# About the author

Kevin McCaffrey is the author of the horror novel *Nightmare Therapy*. He works at Mount Holyoke College in South Hadley, Massachusetts.

CPSIA information can be obtained at www.ICGtesting.com
Printed in the USA
LVOW01n1133160514

386019LV00003B/11/P